D0121028

PRIVATE

photographs by

Alison Jackson

Dedicated to the
memory of my mother

PENGUIN BOOKS

Published by the Penguin Group
Penguin Books Ltd, 80 Strand, London WC2R ORL, England
Penguin Group (USA), Inc., 375 Hudson Street, New York, New York 10014, USA
Penguin Books Australia Ltd, 250 Camberwell Road,
Camberwell, Victoria 3124, Australia
Penguin Books Canada Ltd, 10 Alcorn Avenue, Toronto, Ontario, Canada M4V 3B2
Penguin Books India (P) Ltd, 11 Community Centre,
Panchsheel Park, New Delhi – 110 017, India
Penguin Books (NZ) Ltd, Cnr Rosedale and Airborne Roads,
Albany, Auckland, New Zealand
Penguin Books (South Africa) (Pty) Ltd, 24 Sturdee Avenue,
Rosebank 2196, South Africa

Penguin Books Ltd, Registered Offices: 80 Strand, London WC2R ORL, England

www.penguin.com

First published by Michael Joseph 2003
Published in Penguin Books 2004
1

Copyright © Alison Jackson, 2003
'Miss Dynamite' copyright © Waldemar Januszczak, 2003

Colour Reproduction by Dot Gradations, Wickford, Essex
Printed and bound in Italy by Graphicom

A CIP catalogue record for this book is available from the British Library

Hardly anyone knew Diana. Yet on her death the world mourned. They did not mourn the woman but her photographic image. We all think we know David Beckham; thousands of fans have seen him in the flesh on the pitch, but millions of us know him only through his image. The same goes for all celebrities, whether it's Madonna, Prince William or Tony Blair. The result is that the photograph becomes more real than the actual person or event.

In my work I use celebrity lookalikes to create images which pose fundamental questions about where the truth ends and lies begin. The line between what is real and what is fantasy has never been more blurred. My photographs seek to explore the gap between the two and, if only for a second, bring it sharply into focus.

Alison Jackson

'Profoundly tasteless. What on earth is the matter with people nowadays?' Ann Widdecombe, *Sunday Telegraph*

'Scanning the British art horizon for the descendants of Hogarth, the sons of Goya, the daughters of Dada or the kin of Käthe Kollwitz, for anyone who is willing to pop their head above the parapet and attempt a *Guernica* or a *Death of Marat*, I can only see Alison Jackson' Waldemar Januszczak, *Sunday Times*

'How low can art go?' *Sun*

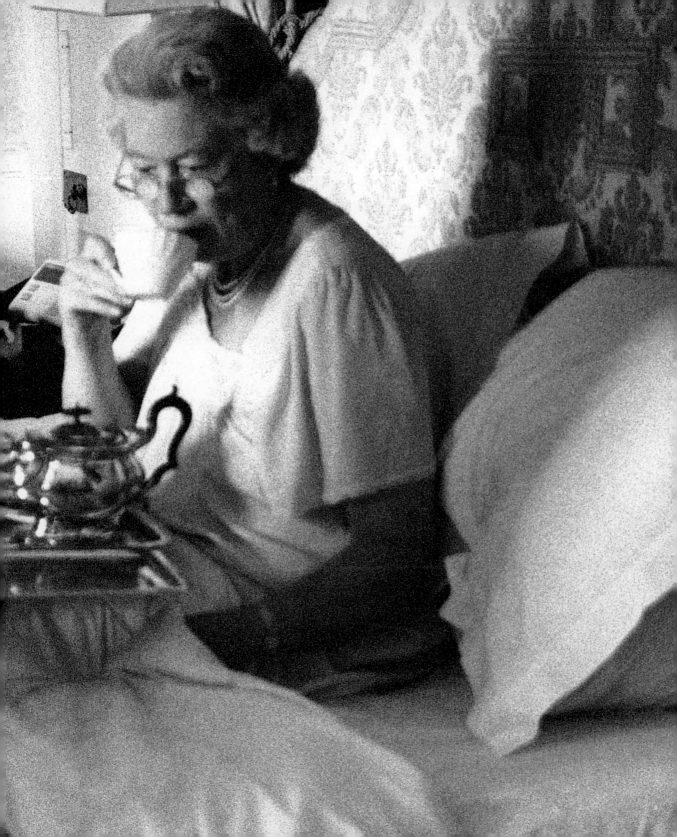

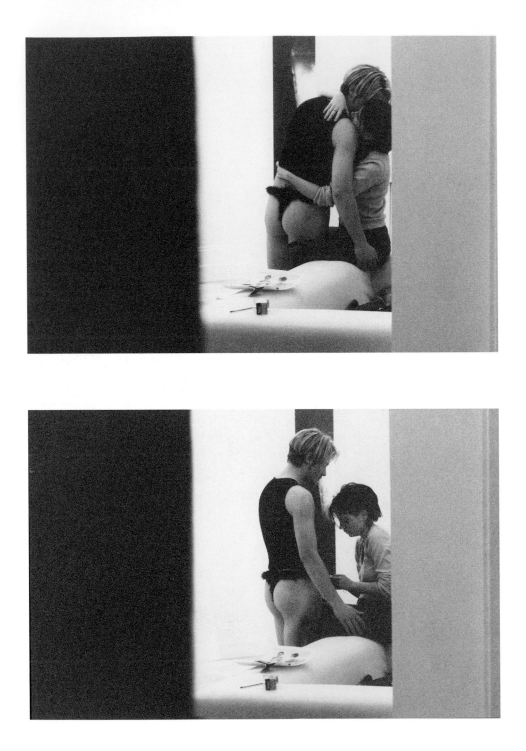

MISS DYNAMITE

Don't make the mistake of thinking you have in your hands a funny book. Sure, one of the things it is is funny. Hilariously, side-splittingly, day-changingly funny on some of its pages. When I first witnessed Sven-Göran Eriksson prancing about in his Union Jack knickers – it was around the time of the last World Cup – I burst into immediate and excellent guffaws. Eriksson's simultaneous entanglement with the lovely Ulrika and the angry Nancy had revealed in him an innate, God-given ridiculousness that Alison Jackson was on to like Owen in the box. I laughed noisily too at the spectacle of Prince William trying on his crown. The heir to the throne must do precisely this, if only in his thoughts. And someone who looks exactly – and I mean exactly – like Tony Blair, horsing around with Cherie's bikini in a swimming pool in Barbados, definitely inspired gulps and giggles. Those extra-brief swimming trunks that the faux Tony was wearing are so terribly, worryingly Tony.

When Alison Jackson gets everything right, her images send irresistible signals to weird nether regions of the brain – located somewhere between the comedy cortex and the cortex that controls cruelty – that immediately trigger these gasps. It's a reflexive thing. Like being tapped on the knee with a hammer. Camilla Parker Bowles posing in the nude for Charles, as Eve, or Philip peering more closely at Marilyn Monroe masturbating, are aggressively hilarious spectacles. We are right to laugh, and we do. But don't, as I said, make the mistake of thinking you have in your hands a funny book or, for that matter, a deliberately rude one. There's stuff going on here that's beyond comedy, way above rudeness. When Alison Jackson gets things exactly right, reality is being successfully tested at its core, its nuclear level.

If these were physics experiments (actually I think they sort of are: the nature of truth is being ascertained), they'd be competing for the Nobel Prize, so entirely convincing are the results. (Sven is Swedish. Maybe he could put in a good word for Alison in Stockholm.) The first of Alison Jackson's reality tests that I encountered is her astonishing image of Lady Di and Dodi Al Fayed showing off their baby, in a Snowdon-photo way. The picture still unsettles me today. All these years after Di and Dodi crashed out of our timescale in that ghastly underpass in Paris, I still can't successfully not-believe this image. I know they are stand-ins. I know it's impossible. But photography exists in the permanent present, and this Di and Dodi, and their gorgeous grinning baby, are absolutely touchable. Deep skill and profound care have gone into the creation of these sensational falsehoods. Jackson goes the extra mile, she's hard-core. And by giving us a Lady Di who is so utterly, faultlessly convincing, she hacks into our sense of reality and tampers with it. The result, this time, isn't one of Alison Jackson's funnies. This is a three-handkerchief weepy. Look at that perfect baby: don't you just want to eat it for its plump-legged, half-Arabic loveableness?

To trust or not to trust? That is the question. After you've had lots and lots of great laughs examining this book, and absorbed some of its superb shocks (the one of the Queen reading on the loo is a killer: look at the pants around her ankles – they're perfect, aren't they?) you may begin to notice patterns emerging. Who are the people whose media-identities are being infiltrated? Well, without exception, they are faces you will recognize. They have to be: otherwise there would be no point. They're members of the royal family, pop stars, football heroes, presidents, prime ministers, leaders of Al Qaeda, dictators, and, in a couple of cases, great dead people of our time. In chat-show terms these are A-list celebs.

But that's not all they share. Every one of these personas has at some point allowed us into their bedrooms, as it were: we've been in the john with them, or between their sheets. Even if the celebs involved were not actually the ones who invited us in, we've already breached their intimacy zone, because, in our world, achieving global recognizability – plucking fame out of the fires of anonymity – involves the signing of a terrible Faustian contract. You get to be rich and famous: we get to own a chunk of you. If you don't like this arrangement, stay anonymous. Don't leave the council estate. Don't go on TV. Remain in Sweden. Don't milk our familiarity. The moment you put your nose above the parapet of fame, part of you belongs to us. Fame is a tap we turn on and off, not you. Otherwise, what's in it for us?

OK, you're the Queen and you're entitled to some privacy. But you're also completely, utterly human, Ma'am, just like us. You do what we do, and it's a lie, a disinfected, dishonest, mutated fantasy, to pretend otherwise. I go to the loo, Your Majesty. You go to the loo. We're family at heart. But to admit to it, Ma'am, to show it, well, that creates frissons. It's an act of rebellion. Treason even. And yet, Ma'am, I doubt whether you have in your kingdom any more loyal and caring subject than this tricky photographer, this magician of image, this sleight-of-hand specialist that is Alison Jackson. If she's on anyone's side it's yours, Ma'am. Because the chief, the great, anomaly in her work is that while pretending to point her camera at this fine assortment of faux celebs – clearly and in Snowdon-style if that's what's called for; but in blurred haste if snapshot speed seems more pertinent – what she is really looking at is us. Our tastes. Our beliefs. Our fascination. Our nosiness. Our chronic reality-slippage. Our contemporary tragedy.

Another pattern: Jackson has a special appetite for broken women. Lady Di we know all about. The picture of Di, Dodi and their baby is a photographic fairy-tale about a princess who beat the system. It only happens in fairy-tales. But look what curious sympathy there also is for the ersatz Camilla Parker Bowles, a middle-aged English rose stuck in the juicy role of a temptress. I adore the fact that Alison Jackson has made something sexy of Camilla: something a prince would want to become a Tampax for. As for Alison Jackson's lightly sagging Marilyn, drinking herself into pleasure, being pawed by presidents, she seems truer to me than the real Marilyn.

So, these are weighty affairs, Swiftian in their satirical intent, Orwellian in their cool savagery. Here are reality tests that trespass on the territory of magic, and, Christ, some of them are uncanny. But that's not necessarily why it's so great to have them. They're great to have because these excellent fictions answer so many of our deepest and dumbest wishes. Who wouldn't want to have been a fly on the wall when Di met Camilla meeting Charles? Who wouldn't want to watch Tony doing the hokey cokey in Barbados, in those trunks? Who wouldn't want to see Diana giving our world the finger? And now we can.

WALDEMAR JANUSZCZAK

Acknowledgements

I should like to thank all the people who have helped and supported me during the making of this work. Particular thanks to:

Lyn and Michael Dyer and all at Michael Dyer Associates for printing and all their extra help.
Design consulting by Beth Derbyshire at Zephyr Projects.
Creative consulting by George Bright.
And special thanks to Paul Arden.

Thanks to Nick Sutherland-Dodd, Katy Niker, Patty Mayer, Mark Lord, Bettina von Hase, Peter Banks, Paul Stevens and Lyndsey Posner at ICM, Susan Scott Agency, Schweppes, Mother – particularly Kim Gehrig and Caroline Pay – John Hamilton and Louise Moore at Penguin, Tiger Aspect, and the BBC for permission to use certain photographs. This work would have been impossible without the skill of my hair and make-up team: Sue Daniels, Heather Squire and Linda McKnight; and the production and post-production team: Derek Frost, Brian Voce and Jessica Fulford-Dobson. Thanks also to Tina Pelini, whose skill as a photographic model has led to her inclusion in most of the photographs.

And, of course, a big thank-you to all the lookalikes.

Finally, thank you to Richard Salmon and Sotoris Kyriacou at the
Richard Salmon Gallery, 59 South Edwardes Square, London, W8 6HW.

Self-portrait of the artist 2003 Alison Jackson

Alison Jackson is the award-winning artist who created the BBC TV series *Double Take* and the internationally acclaimed Schweppes advertising campaign. After studying sculpture and then Fine Art Photography at the Royal College of Art in London, Alison's work has, for the last five years, astonished and sometimes shocked audiences on both sides of the Atlantic.

Alison Jackson exhibits in museums and art galleries worldwide. Fittingly for an artist concerned conceptually with blurring boundaries, she communicates her ideas across a range of disciplines. She has contributed to several books and given lectures and workshops at Tate Britain, the ICA, the National Portrait Gallery and the Edinburgh TV Festival, amongst others, as well as at various educational establishments. She won a BAFTA for Innovation for her TV show *Double Take*, and other awards include a Photographers Gallery Award, Gold and several Silver Advertising Awards and a Best of the Best Award from Alan Parker.

Alison Jackson lives in London next door to a team of lawyers and bears no resemblance whatsoever to anybody famous.